Not on Earth!

However, there are some theories that suggest that life didn't begin on Earth at all! Some scientists think that the molecules on which life is based may have arrived from another planet on a meteorite or a comet.

Researchers have found evidence of these molecules on one of Jupiter's moons and on asteroids. We may never know exactly how life on Earth began, but we know now exactly how to decide if something is a living organism or not. Turn the page to find out more.

Jupiter

Meet Mrs Gren

So, what *is* life? There are some quite complicated explanations of the characteristics of life, (processes that every single living thing carries out) but we'll stick to the simple ones, and our guide will be Mrs Gren. Who on earth is Mrs Gren? She's just a handy way of remembering the first letters of the seven basic characteristics of life!

Movement
Reproduction
Sensitivity
Growth
Respiration
Excretion
Nutrition

Movement

This can mean a number of things; movement within a single cell, movement of parts of an animal or plant, or locomotion (the ability to move from place to place). There's a tiny transport system inside every cell, which moves materials to where they are needed, and even animals that spend all their lives in one place can move parts of their bodies.

For instance, sea anemones are stuck to rocks in the sea, but can move their tentacles. Most animals move from place to place, and they use lots of different methods to do so: swimming, crawling, walking, running, jumping, swinging, flying.

But even if things move around inside their cells, plants don't move – or do they? They don't usually move from place to place, but they *do* move. It's just that they do it so slowly that it's hard for us to notice.

There are exceptions though – the Venus flytrap has special pairs of leaves that close very fast if an insect walks over them, and the 'sensitive plant' closes its delicate leaves in the rain.

Reproduction

This is the process of producing offspring (new organisms). This allows species to survive for millions of years. Very simple organisms like bacteria just split in two; in some plants a piece can break off and grow into a whole new individual. This is called *asexual reproduction*. However, most plants and animals use *sexual reproduction*. This involves two special cells – one from the male parent and one from the female parent – joining together.

Sensitivity

No, not bursting into tears! This means the ability to respond to changes in the environment or inside the organism itself. Plant shoots grow towards light, and their roots grow towards gravity. Animals use their senses to detect food and predators. You respond to changes in temperature by shivering or sweating. Organisms also respond to changes *inside* their own bodies; for instance, your brain is constantly altering your heartbeat and breathing rate to keep conditions perfect for your cells.

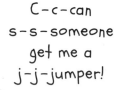

C–c–can s–s–someone get me a j–j–jumper!

9

Growth

Huge oak trees begin as small acorns, humans start as a single cell the size of a full stop, kangaroos are born about the size of a jelly bean… Everything grows. Animals get to a certain size and stop, but many plants keep growing all through their lifetime. Growth is an *irreversible* increase in size or mass. If you drink 500 millilitres of water, you will gain 500 grams in mass, but you haven't grown as the change is reversible and you'll get rid of the water later.

I wonder will I grow to be that big?

Respiration

To a scientist, this doesn't mean breathing. Ever wondered why you need to eat? This is how your body gets the raw materials it needs for growth and repair, but food is also the fuel you use to give your body energy to do everything. Respiration is how cells break down chemicals like glucose sugar to release the energy they contain. It's a bit like burning oil or wood to release energy as heat and light, but of course there aren't tiny fires burning in your cells! Instead, the energy is released in a much slower, more controlled way.

Excretion

This is the act of getting rid of waste products that have been made by an organism. Lots of chemical reactions take place in every living cell. Some of these create substances that aren't needed or might be toxic. For example, most cells produce carbon dioxide gas when they respire (break down chemicals), and you excrete this every time you breathe out. Water is produced as a waste product in many reactions inside the body and when animals break down protein they produce toxic substances. Both of these are excreted in urine.

Nutrition

As far as animals are concerned, this means eating, whether it's a slice of chocolate cake for you, a blood meal for a flea, or some delicious rotting meat for a maggot! Plants make their own food, by a process called photosynthesis. Using a special molecule called chlorophyll (which is what gives them their green colour) they can use the energy in sunlight to build up carbon dioxide gas and water into sugar. Imagine if we could do that… we'd get fat in summer when it was sunny, and thin in winter when it was gloomy. And we'd be green, of course!

Cells

All living things are made of cells, but what exactly *is* a cell? No one knew they existed until in the 1600s Robert Hooke invented a microscope that could magnify things so they looked 50 times larger than they actually were. He looked at a very thin slice of cork and saw it was made of tiny walled spaces. These reminded him of the cells in which monks lived and the name *cell* stuck.

● There are two basic types of cell. *Prokaryotic cells* are very simple, and are only found in bacteria. *Eukaryotic cells* are much more complex, and make up everything from the single-celled fungus yeast, to humans.

● Plant and animal cells are different from each other too.

Robert Hooke.

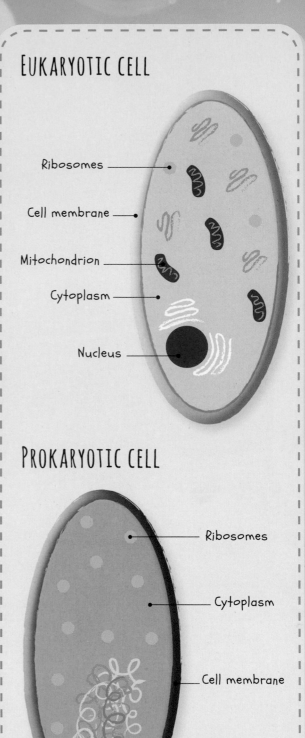

Eukaryotic Cell

Ribosomes

Cell membrane

Mitochondrion

Cytoplasm

Nucleus

Prokaryotic Cell

Ribosomes

Cytoplasm

Cell membrane

Free DNA
(no nucleus)

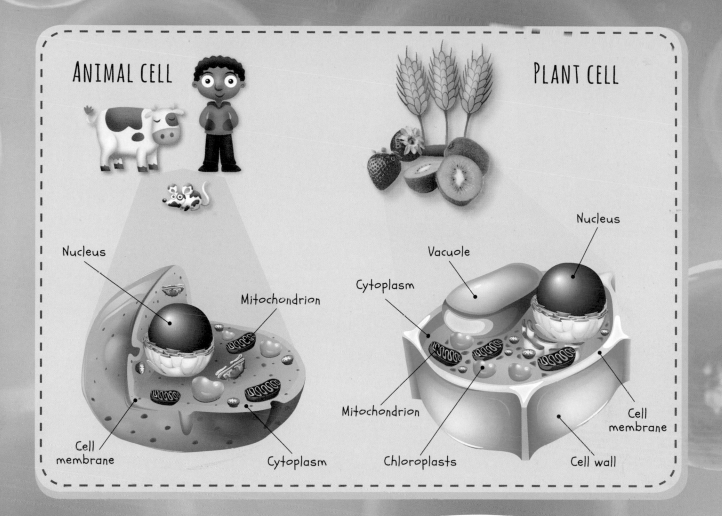

ANIMAL CELL

Nucleus

Mitochondrion

Cell membrane

Cytoplasm

PLANT CELL

Nucleus

Vacuole

Cytoplasm

Mitochondrion

Chloroplasts

Cell wall

Cell membrane

Cell jobs

There are lots of variations on the basic cell plan, all with different jobs to do. For example animals have nerve cells that may be more than a metre long, red blood cells that have no nucleus, brain cells that each communicate with 10,000 others, and white blood cells that crawl through their bodies searching for bacteria. Plant cells are adapted to make food, take in water, sting, support the plant, and transport substances up and down the stem.

And I thought cells were just tiny blobs!

Single-celled organisms

Many living things manage to carry out all the Mrs Gren characteristics in one single cell. Some of these organisms are like tiny animals, and others are like minute plants. However, not all of them are easy to categorise: for instance, there's one type of organism that has chlorophyll (like a plant), and a simple eye (like an animal).

Sponge soup? Do I eat it or have a bath in it?

Multicellular organisms

Most organisms – humans, for instance – are made up of many millions of cells working together. In these multicellular organisms, there are lots of different types of cell, each with a special job to do. Some of the simplest multicellular organisms are sponges. They only have a few types of cell, but they don't need to be more complex as all they do is sit on a rock, let water flow through them, and filter out tiny particles of food. Amazingly, if you push a sponge through a sieve so that you basically have sponge soup, and leave it for a while, the individual cells will join together again to reform the sponge!

Natural sponges.

14

Slime moulds

Even stranger are the slime moulds. They live most of their lives as single cells, but if food runs out, they release chemicals that let them find other slime mould cells and join up to form a multicellular phase called a slug (not like the ones in your garden though). The slug slithers along until it comes to open ground, then the cells climb up each other to form something like a tiny mushroom.

Some of the cells turn into spores and float away. This is how the mould reproduces. The ones that formed the 'stalk' of the mushroom die. Scientists have found that slime moulds can solve mazes! Remember, this is something without a head, never mind a brain!

Slime moulds join together to make something like a tiny mushroom.

Organising Organisms

If aliens arrived on Earth and took samples of every living thing, they'd have a very big heap of organisms to sort out (and they'd need a very big spaceship). They would sort them by looking at resemblances and differences and gradually put them all into groups. Scientists on Earth have already done this for the species they know about. The process is called Classification.

Classification

The first attempts to do this sorted everything into two 'heaps', or **Kingdoms**: Plants and Animals. However, as scientists learned more about the organisms they were studying, they realised that not everything fitted into these groups.

The system most commonly used now has five Kingdoms: Bacteria, Protists, Fungi, Plants and Animals. These five Kingdoms are the most basic divisions. By comparing the features of different organisms within the same Kingdom, scientists can divide each Kingdom into smaller and smaller groups with more features in common. The smallest groups are called **Species**. The next page shows how each group is divided down into a smaller category.

→ Each Kingdom is divided into → Phyla

→ Each Phylum is divided into → Classes

→ Each Class is divided into → Orders

→ Each Order is divided into → Families

→ Each Family is divided into → Genera

→ Each Genus is divided into → Species

Below is an example of the groups, from largest to smallest, showing how humans are classified:

LARGEST GROUP

The organisms in it have a few basic features in common. Contains every single animal.

SMALLEST GROUP

Every organism of the same species has lots of features in common. All the animals in the species Homo sapiens are humans. →

Groups	Human Classification
Kingdom	Animals
Phylum	Chordates
Class	Mammals
Order	Primates
Family	Hominids
Genus	Homo
Species	Sapiens

Naming Organisms

For centuries, people gave local names to plants and animals. This was very confusing as it meant the same plant could end up with many different names. For instance, foxgloves were also called 'dead man's bells', 'fairy thimbles' and 'witch's gloves' and it became very difficult for scientists from different areas to be sure they were all talking about the same plant. Someone needed to sort things out: enter Carl Linnaeus!

Carl Linnaeus.

Linnaeus takes charge

Linnaeus was a Swedish botanist who decided that a new naming system was badly needed. He turned to Latin for help. During the 18th century, Latin was the language of learning. If you went to any university, in any European country, you had to know Latin. Linnaeus came up with a system where every living thing would have a two-part Latin name that would be agreed on and used by scientists everywhere.

Linnaeus' System

For example, the foxglove is called *Digitalis purpurea* and humans are *Homo sapiens*. The first bit of the name is the genus (a bit like the surname) and the second bit is the species (a bit like a first name). Very closely related organisms share their genus name – *Homo neanderthalensis* is Neanderthal man, the nearest relative to modern humans, and there are over 20 *Digitalis* species.

More than just names...

The other clever thing about these names is that most of them describe something about the organism. *Digitalis* means 'finger-like' and the flowers of a foxglove fit perfectly onto your fingers (but not so well onto a fox's paw) and *purpurea* means 'purple'. In *Homo sapiens*, *Homo* means 'man' and *sapiens* means 'wise'. *Neanderthalensis* refers to where the first fossils were found – the Neander valley in Germany.

Now we've looked at the basics, let's start our beginner's tour of life on Earth!

The Five Kingdoms

The Five Kingdoms are the biggest of the groups into which all living organisms are classified. The organisms in each Kingdom share some basic features. But there's one group that doesn't fit anywhere...

> Wow! that virus looks like a space craft!

Viruses

This is a group that made scientists who were classifying things scratch their heads. A virus isn't a cell – it's just a bit of DNA wrapped up in protein. Everything else with DNA is a living thing, but everything else with DNA is made of cells. New viruses get made, so surely that's reproduction?

In fact, viruses can only get themselves reproduced if they hijack a living cell to do it for them. They are *not* living things. They seem to have *some* of the Mrs Gren characteristics, but a living organism has to have *all* of them, *and* be made of cells.

Diseases

All viruses cause diseases because they destroy cells when they use them to make new viruses. Some of these diseases are mild, like the common cold, but others like smallpox and HIV (Human Immunodeficiency Virus, which causes AIDS) are deadly.

However, they're not all bad. There is a group of viruses called bacteriophages which only target bacteria. Some bacteria cause diseases, so perhaps we can use these viruses to kill them and prevent those diseases.

Bacteriophage.

The Protists Kingdom

This is a very mixed group. It's like that cupboard where you put things that don't quite belong anywhere else: living things that aren't animals, plants, fungi or bacteria end up in this Kingdom

Lots of protists are single celled organisms found in water. If you collect water from a pond and look at it under a microscope – or even a good magnifying glass – you'll see lots of them.

Amoeba proteus, under a microscope.

Malaria

Some protists cause diseases. Malaria is caused by a protist called *Plasmodium*, carried and spread by some types of mosquitoes. When they bite, they inject the *Plasmodium* into their victim's blood. Malaria affects around two million people every year and kills around 500,000.

21

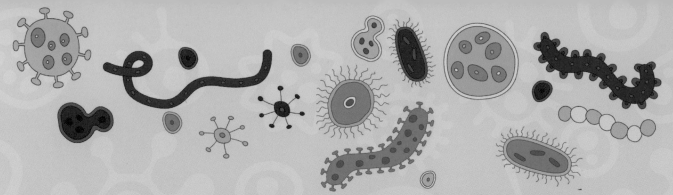

The Bacteria Kingdom

You're probably thinking "*Urgh – germs*", but you shouldn't. Most bacteria are harmless, and some are actually very helpful.

Each bacterium is a single prokaryotic cell. They are the simplest forms of life and they exist almost everywhere, including all over you! Your skin is covered in them, no matter how clean you are, and your guts are full of them too.

In fact, you contain more bacteria than human cells! The ones in your gut help you process food, and if they all get destroyed, it can make you feel quite ill. The ones on your skin don't do any harm, although some of them might if they get into a wound.

Here are a few stars of the bacteria world:

◉ *Lactobacillus*: Very useful to humans who like cheese and yoghurt, because it is this bacterium that changes milk into those products.

◉ *Geobacter*: This can gobble up pollutants from oil spills. Even better, it may be able to use wastes like compost to generate electricity, acting as a living battery.

◉ *Decomposers*: When organisms die, they are usually decomposed (broken down into simple substances) by bacteria (and fungi). If this didn't happen, we'd be hip-deep in dead dinosaurs and daisies, and there would be no nutrients put back into the environment to make new organisms.

And some of the nasties:

◉ *Yersinia pestis:* This causes the Bubonic Plague, which was known as The Black Death in medieval times. It killed over one third of the population of Europe (about 200 million people) during the 14th century.

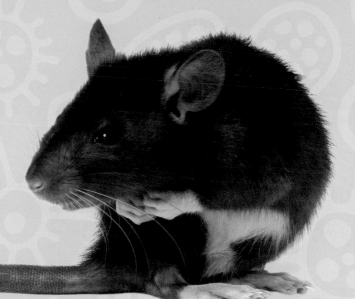

Fleas on rats spread the Bubonic Plague during the 14ᵗʰ century.

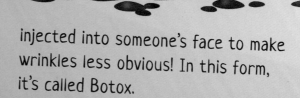

◉ *Clostridium botulinum:* This lives in soil, but occasionally makes its way into damaged tins of food. It makes the most toxic substance of any living thing — botulinum toxin. This is so toxic that a teaspoonful in a reservoir supplying water to a major city would be enough to kill everyone in the city who drank it, and a kilogram (the weight of a bag of sugar) could kill every animal in the world. If it is greatly diluted however, it can be injected into someone's face to make wrinkles less obvious! In this form, it's called Botox.

The Fungi Kingdom

For hundreds of years, people thought of fungi as plants. It made sense: they grew in the ground, they didn't move around, and they didn't seem to eat. But in fact, fungi are very, very different from plants.

The biggest difference is that they can't make their own food. Instead, they make digestive liquids and use them to dissolve dead organisms. This means that, like bacteria, they are important in decomposition. Some of this is useful, but it can be harmful too. Mildew can spoil books and clothes, and athlete's foot is a fungus that loves to chomp on damp, dead skin between your toes.

When you think of fungi, you probably think of the mushrooms you can eat, but that's not what all fungi look like. Some are single cells. Yeast, for example, which helps bread to rise. It does this when it carries out respiration.

The carbon dioxide yeast produces makes the bread dough rise before baking.

24

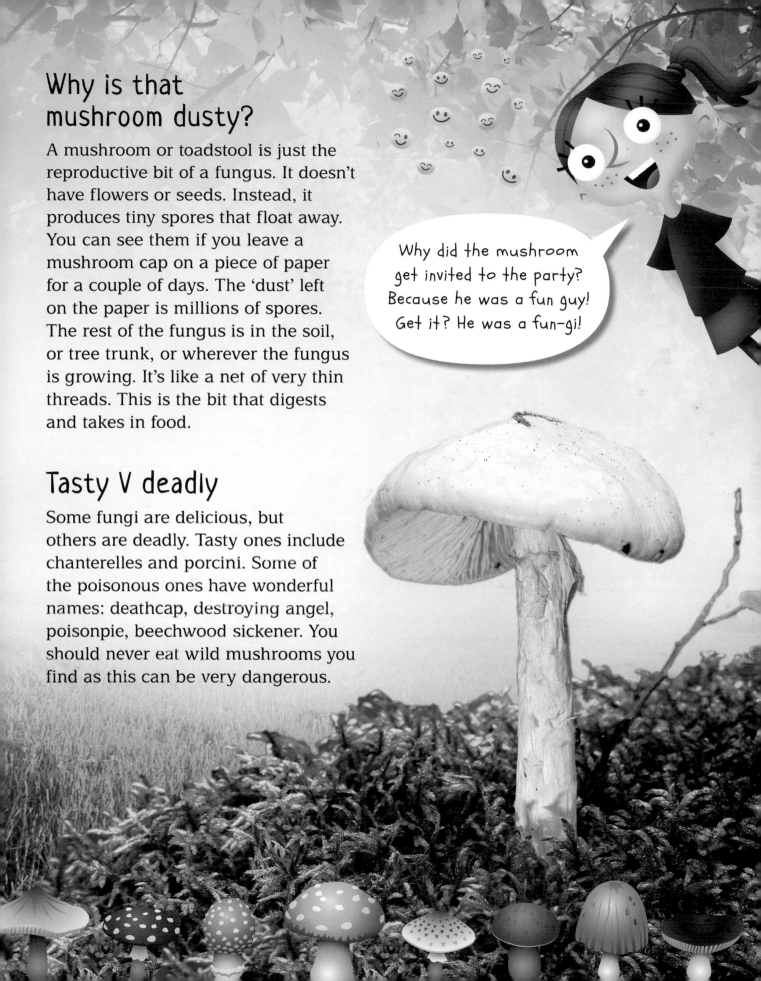

Why is that mushroom dusty?

A mushroom or toadstool is just the reproductive bit of a fungus. It doesn't have flowers or seeds. Instead, it produces tiny spores that float away. You can see them if you leave a mushroom cap on a piece of paper for a couple of days. The 'dust' left on the paper is millions of spores. The rest of the fungus is in the soil, or tree trunk, or wherever the fungus is growing. It's like a net of very thin threads. This is the bit that digests and takes in food.

Why did the mushroom get invited to the party? Because he was a fun guy! Get it? He was a fun-gi!

Tasty V deadly

Some fungi are delicious, but others are deadly. Tasty ones include chanterelles and porcini. Some of the poisonous ones have wonderful names: deathcap, destroying angel, poisonpie, beechwood sickener. You should never eat wild mushrooms you find as this can be very dangerous.

The Plant Kingdom

Lots of people think plants are boring and that they don't do anything but they couldn't be more wrong. Life in the plant world is just as dramatic and cut-throat as the Animal Kingdom; it's just that to us, it seems to take place in slow motion but there are killers, kidnappers, frauds...

Nutrition

Plants contain a green pigment called chlorophyll. This allows them to make their own food from carbon dioxide and water using the energy in sunlight. They can absorb the other minerals they need through their roots. Almost every other living thing depends on plants' ability to photosynthesise, either because they eat plants, or they eat animals that eat plants.

Plants that live in waterlogged soil – in bogs, for instance – can have trouble getting enough nitrogen. They solve this by becoming killers.

Killers

These are the insectivorous plants like Venus flytraps and pitcher plants. Venus flytraps have special pairs of leaves with sensitive hairs on them. If an insect touches three of these hairs, the leaf trap closes quickly, and the more the insect struggles, the tighter it closes. Once it has trapped something, the leaves produce liquid that digests the insect's body, and the plant absorbs the nutrients.

Pitcher plants attract flies by releasing a smell like dead meat. The inside of the pitcher (a modified leaf) is very slippery and the shape makes it difficult for the flies to get out. If they fall into the pool of digestive liquid at the bottom they meet their doom.

Growth

Different plants grow at different rates and to different heights. The fastest growing plants are bamboos – some of them can grow more than a metre a day!

The largest plant in the world is 'General Sherman' a giant sequoia tree in California. It is almost 88 metres tall and 7.7 metres in diameter.

One of the slowest growing plants is *Puya raimondii*, which normally lives high in the Bolivian mountains and can take 80–100 years to grow big enough to flower. Another is the Saguaro cactus (which you often see in the background of Western films). It can live for 200 years, but might only be three centimetres tall after the first ten years, and only grows two to three centimetres per year.

Plant reproduction

Many, but not all, plants reproduce by using flowers to make male pollen and female ovules. These have to be transferred from one flower to another for fertilisation to take place and seeds to be formed. Some flowering plants just rely on the wind to blow their pollen to another flower, while others rely on insects, birds, bats, mice and even lizards to carry the pollen from one flower to the other. Some plants use bribery to attract creatures, making sweet sugary nectar for them to drink. Other plants play tricks...

Kidnappers

The giant water lily kidnaps beetles. If they crawl into a lily flower, attracted by a pineapple-like scent, the flower shuts round them in the evening. The next day, when they are finally allowed to leave, they are covered in pollen, and when they visit another lily flower the pollen rubs off them and fertilises the ovules. Once the flower has released the beetle it closes up and sinks down into the water.

Frauds

Hammer orchids are the frauds of the plant world and have flowers that look and smell like the flightless females of a species of wasp. The male wasp comes along looking for love and tries to carry off a mate but instead another bit of the flower hits him on the head and covers him in pollen. The male wasp flies to the next flower with its pretend female wasp and when he gets hit again, the pollen he is carrying gets transferred to the second flower.

What does he get out of this? Nothing (except possibly a headache).

Sensitivity

Plants are most sensitive to light, and will change their direction of growth so that their leaves get as much light as possible. You see this happen if you keep a plant by a window: it becomes bent towards the light. They are also sensitive to gravity and this is why roots always grow down and shoots always grow up. If they couldn't do this, you would have to make sure every seed you planted was the right way up! Some plants are sensitive to touch, like the Venus flytrap and the 'sensitive plant'. Plants like bindweed, peas and beans will twine round anything they touch. This allows them to grow higher without needing a really strong stem of their own.

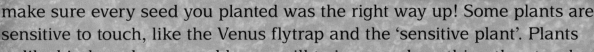

The Animal Kingdom

This covers everything from sponges to humans. There are quite a lot of different types of organisms in the Animal Kingdom so to avoid any confusion let's break them down further and look at each of the main phyla one by one (the phyla are the smaller groups into which the Kingdoms are divided – turn to page 17 for more on how organisms are organised).

Phylum: Cnidaria

These include jellyfish, sea anemones and corals, and most of them live in the sea. They have very simple bodies – no head, arms, legs, brain or heart – but they do have tentacles with stinging cells which they use to catch their food. Jellyfish range from the peanut-sized and deadly venomous Irukandji to the huge lion's mane, which can be the size of a small car!

Corals are tiny animals that live in huge colonies. Many have a stony external skeleton, and these build up over many years to form coral reefs like the Great Barrier Reef.

Phylum: Flatworms

These are simple, soft-bodied worms, with one opening that doubles as a mouth and an anus. The group includes lots of worms you don't want to meet, like tapeworms, blood flukes and New Zealand flatworms.

Tapeworms live in the guts of mammals. In humans they can grow to ten metres long. You get them by eating undercooked meat that contains their eggs. Not all flatworms are harmful though. If you have a pond, look carefully at the bottom, and you might see small harmless flatworms 5-10 millimetres long gliding around. These are called planarians. When you look at these through a magnifying glass you can see tiny spots at the front end – these are very simple eyes, which can tell light from dark, but not much else.

Phylum: Echinoderms

This is the group where you find starfish, sea urchins and sea cucumbers. They have a separate mouth and anus, but no head, or circulatory system.

They all live in the sea and have what's called radial symmetry – they are shaped a bit like a pie you could cut into identical wedges.

A 'basic' starfish has five arms, with lots of feet on each arm, so it can creep around the seabed, eating. If one of their arms gets damaged, they can grow an new one!

Sea urchins and cucumbers

Sea urchins and sea cucumbers don't look as if they are closely related to starfish. Try to imagine a starfish that's put all its arms together above its middle so it's pumpkin-shaped for a sea urchin, and then stretched out to be as long as possible for a sea cucumber.

Sea cucumbers have a strange way of defending themselves if something tries to eat them. They throw up what's in their gut, along with their whole gut as well! This sticks all over whatever is attacking them, giving them time to creep away, but leaving them with a problem. How do you eat when your gut is gone? Here's the really clever bit – they grow a new one!

Phylum: Roundworms

Flatworms are flat and roundworms are – yes, you guessed – round. They are more complicated than flatworms, as they have a nervous system but no circulatory system.

   Some of them are parasites and live in the guts of animals like cats, dogs, humans and whales (whale ones are several metres long). Roundworms, sometimes called nematodes, can also be pests in plants, and live in soil in huge numbers. There may be hundreds in one kilogram of soil, but they are so small that you need a microscope to see most of them.

A giant Australian worm can live up to 20 years!

Phylum: Annelids

This is where scientists file earthworms, leeches and other segmented worms (segments are repeated units – like the segments of an orange. Each segment of a worm has the same basic structures inside). They have a proper gut, a nervous system and a circulatory system.

Earthworm.

Earthworms

Did you know that soil is basically earthworm droppings? They eat dead and decaying leaves, and when they get rid of the waste, it forms soil. Their burrows also help drainage, so if you want good soil, you need earthworms. The biggest ones are found in Australia, and can be over three metres long!

Leeches

Leeches live in water or in very damp places. Some are predators, but many are parasites, which feed by sucking blood from other animals. There are lots of leech species that feed on fish blood, but some target birds or mammals – including humans. They can survive for a year on a single blood meal. When a leech bites it injects a local anaesthetic so the animal doesn't feel the bite, and it also injects an anticoagulant chemical to stop the blood clotting. Crafty!

Leech medicine

For hundreds of years leeches were used in medicine, because doctors thought a lot of diseases could be cured by bleeding people. They were wrong, of course, and the practice died out. However, leeches are being used in modern surgery. They're the best way to keep blood flowing through a reattached finger after surgery – and new anticoagulant drugs based on leeches have been developed.

Small garden snail.

Phylum: Molluscs

Molluscs have soft, squashy bodies, and many of them have a shell which protects them. They have a heart and circulatory system and a complex nervous system. Most, but not all, live in water. They include snails and slugs, mussels and oysters, octopus and squid.

Snails and slugs are very similar; snails have shells they can retreat into and slugs don't. They have tongues that are rough, a bit like a nail file, and eat by scraping away at plant leaves. The biggest one is the giant African land snail, which can weigh up to one kilogram.

Snails

Snails are hermaphrodites, which means each snail is male and female at the same time. You might think that means it just takes one snail to reproduce, but you still need two.

To decide who's going to do what they shoot love darts at each other. These are tiny spikes which mating snails try to stab into each other. The one who stabs first is more likely to end up as the male in the mating process. And you thought snails were boring!

Some gardeners put copper stripes around plant pots to keep snails away. It works because the copper gives snails an electric shock!

Giant African land snail.

34

Bivalves

A bivalve is a mollusc with a pair of shells and there are over 10,000 species – cockles, mussels and oysters are just a few. Some live in freshwater, but most are found in the sea. When they are underwater, their shells are open, water flows through them and they filter out tiny bits of food. If oysters or mussels get a bit of grit stuck in them, they produce a substance called nacre and wrap the grit in it to protect themselves from irritation. Layers of nacre build up to form a pearl.

Unlike snails and slugs, bivalves don't have a head and they don't move around as adults. To reproduce they release lots of gametes into the sea, and it's just a matter of luck if two of the same species meet up. If they do, they produce a tiny larva that swims around until it finds the right sort of rock, where it settles down for the rest of its life.

Ming the clam was probably the oldest animal in the world, until scientists accidentally killed him. He lived on the seabed near Iceland and was at least 500 years old when an attempt to calculate his age by counting the rings on his shell killed him.

Octopus, squid and cuttlefish

Octopus have eight arms and squid and cuttlefish have ten. If they are threatened, they shoot a cloud of black ink into the water to confuse their predators and then escape by jet-propelling themselves with a blast of water. Their skin can change colour and pattern very quickly. They use this to communicate and to camouflage themselves. Mimic octopuses use this along with an ability to change their body shape, to pretend to be completely different animals! Octopus can also use tools. They can unscrew a lid to get at prey, hide under shells and solve mazes.

Phylum: Arthropods

This is the largest and most important invertebrate phylum, so we'll look at it class by class (remember, each phylum is divided into classes). The four classes are Insects, Arachnids, Myriapods and Crustaceans.

Class: Insects

Insects have six legs and bodies divided into three parts: head, thorax and abdomen. Many, but not all of them, have two pairs of wings. Insects are the most successful and widespread animal group on Earth, with at least one million species.

From the biggest...
To the smallest...

The biggest insect is probably the Goliath beetle, which weighs 115 grams and can grow to be 11.5 centimetres long. The longest insects are stick insects; the record is 56.7 centimetres.

The largest butterfly in the world is the Queen Alexandra's birdwing, with a wingspan of 28 centimetres. But there are some very small insects too.

28cm wingspam

The smallest ones are the fairyflies, which are actually tiny wasps, and can be as small as 0.14 millimetres in length. That's smaller than some single-celled organisms and yet they have digestive, reproductive, circulatory and nervous systems packed in there.

Small but deadly...

Some insects can be extremely dangerous. Mosquitoes kill millions of people by transmitting malaria; fleas transmitted the bacteria of the Bubonic Plague, while tsetse flies spread sleeping sickness that kills hundreds of thousands of people in Africa every year.

Long distance travellers

Insects can travel great distances — The Monarch butterfly moves about 7,000 kilometres in an annual migration from Mexico to Southern Canada and back. However, it takes four generations of butterfly to do this. The globe skimmer dragonfly may have that beaten by a long way: it looks as though it migrates from southern India to southern Africa, and back again — that's 14,000 kilometres — also taking four generations to do it.

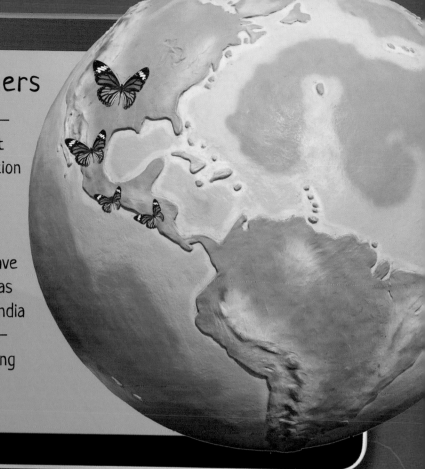

Did you know there are over 350,000 different species of beetle in the world?

Class: Arachnids

Arachnids have four pairs of legs and include spiders, mites and scorpions.

Spiders

House spiders are harmless and helpful, eating all sorts of potentially annoying insects. However, spiders in certain countries can be quite hazardous: the bites of the black widow and redback spider can be fatal.

Spider silk is produced by organs called spinnerets at the back of the abdomen and is used by spiders to make webs, nets, nests and cocoons. It is one of the strongest substances in the world for its weight. Researchers are extremely interested in it and have genetically modified bacteria, plants and even goats to be able to produce it! A cape made of spider silk took three years and the silk from over one million Golden Orb spiders to produce.

Mites

You might not have ever seen a mite before, but if you have a pet dog or cat that scratches its ears a lot, it may have mites in them. If you have asthma, this may be triggered by the droppings of house dust mites.

Some mites have very strange life cycles. The strangest of all is *Acarophenax tribolii*. Fifteen eggs develop and hatch inside the female mite. One is male and the others are all female. The male mates with all his sisters and promptly dies. The females, each now containing 15 developing eggs, eat their way out of their mother – while she's still alive – and the whole cycle begins again!

Scorpions

Scorpions have a very distinctive body shape. They have large front claws, four pairs of walking legs and a curving, venomous stinger, but did you know they also glow in the dark? Their cuticle (outer covering) is fluorescent under UV light, although it looks black in daylight.

Out of around 1,000 species of scorpions, only 25 have venom that is deadly to humans, though many of the others would cause a lot of pain.

Generally scorpions with big claws and small stingers aren't very venomous, but if they have small claws and a big stinger they are. Scorpion venoms are now being investigated for medical use.

Scorpion under UV light.

Class: Myriapods

There are two types of Myriapods – centipedes and millipedes. These are animals with lots of body segments and even more legs. How many legs does a myriapod have? It depends… The fewest has ten, the most has around 750!

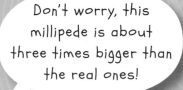

Don't worry, this millipede is about three times bigger than the real ones!

Millipedes

Millipedes have two pairs of legs on each body segment. They don't tend to be as fast moving as centipedes but they don't have to be, as they eat plants, not other animals. The largest known one measured over 37 centimetres.

Centipedes

Centipedes are fast on their numerous feet. They have to be, since they are predators – many have a venomous bite. The biggest one can be more than 30 centimetres long. They have one pair of legs on each of their body segments.

Class: Crustaceans

Shrimps, prawns, lobsters, crabs and woodlice are all crustaceans. Woodlice are the odd ones out here as they are the only members of this group that live on land. You can find them in your garden, under flower pots or bits of rotting wood. All the others live in the sea or fresh water.

Woodlice are crustaceans which live on land.

Barnacles

Barnacles spend all of their adult life in a shell, stuck to a rock, standing on their heads kicking food into their mouths. They are the white, crusty things found on rocks at the seaside, but they will also grow on the underside of boats, and even on the skin of whales! This doesn't harm the whale – its skin is so thick that it doesn't even notice – but some crustaceans are parasites.

The nastiest one is the tongue-eating louse. This horrible parasite gets into a fish through its gills, attaches itself to the fish's tongue and extracts the blood from it with its claws, then takes the place of the tongue once it has been destroyed.

Barnacles might be one of the oldest surviving creatures on the planet and it's thought they haven't changed very much over that time.

40

How big?

Crustaceans come in many different sizes. Horseshoe crabs can be up to 60 centimetres long and the giant amphipod – a deep sea version of a woodlouse – can be 45 centimetres long! Imagine if that was in your back garden, not deep in the sea!

The smallest crustacean is *Stygotantulus stocki*. It is less than 0.1 millimetres long and lives as a parasite on other small crustaceans.

Mantis shrimp.

Horseshoe crab.

Super shrimps

One of the most impressive crustaceans has to be the mantis shrimp. Mantis shrimp have the most complex eyes of any animal. They can see in the UV and infra red parts of the spectrum, as well as in normal light. Their front legs are adapted into spears or clubs (depending on species), and they can whack their prey with enough force to shatter the glass in an aquarium tank.

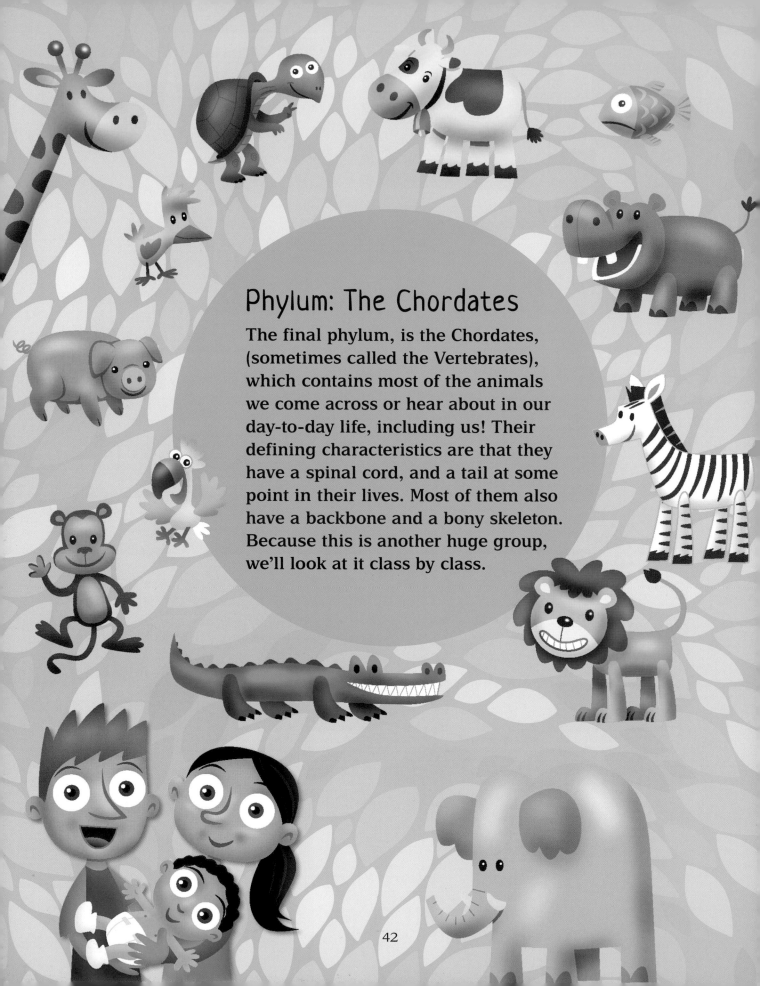

Phylum: The Chordates

The final phylum, is the Chordates, (sometimes called the Vertebrates), which contains most of the animals we come across or hear about in our day-to-day life, including us! Their defining characteristics are that they have a spinal cord, and a tail at some point in their lives. Most of them also have a backbone and a bony skeleton. Because this is another huge group, we'll look at it class by class.

Class: Fish

To qualify as a fish, you need to live in water, swim using muscles and fins, be covered in scales, breathe using gills and lay eggs in water.

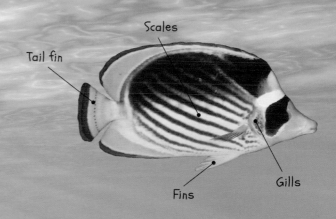

Scales

Tail fin

Fins

Gills

Sharks

Sharks are fish, but their skeletons are made of cartilage (like the wobbly stuff at the end of your nose) and they have rough skin instead of scales. There are over 400 species of shark, from the small zebra shark, gentle enough to share an aquarium with other fish, to the great white, which will attack almost anything, including people; from the whale shark, the world's largest fish, to the basking shark, which must have one of the world's largest mouths, to the deeply strange goblin and hammerhead sharks.

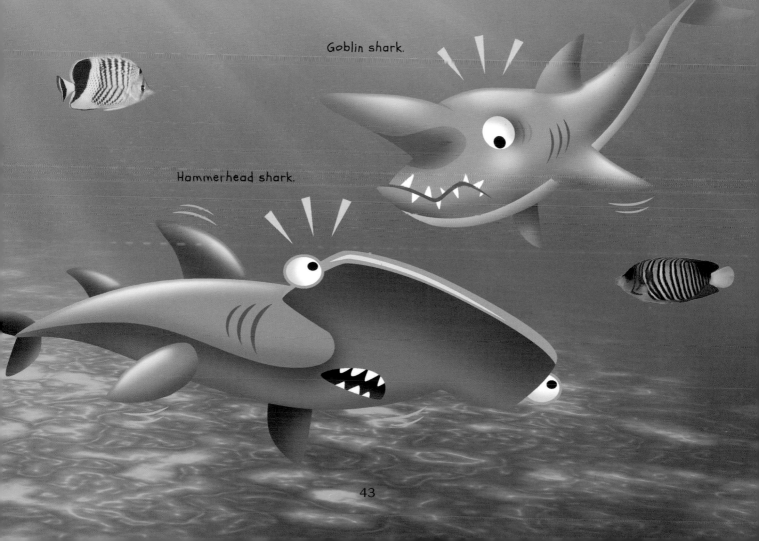

Goblin shark.

Hammerhead shark.

Fresh or salt?

A goldfish is a good example of a fish that lives in fresh water. If you've heard the phrase 'to drink like a fish' it might be a bit of a surprise to learn that freshwater fish don't drink at all. Ever. This is because they take in water all over their body surface, and their problem is getting it out again so in order to do so they pee a lot.

Fish that live in the sea *lose* water all the time, so they do drink, and pee as little as possible. Haddock and cod – which you have probably eaten if you like fish and chips – are good examples of sea fish.

Some fish, like salmon and eels, live part of their lives in fresh water and part in the sea, and have to undergo a sort of Clark-Kent-to-Superman change when they move from one to the other.

Amazing eels

In estuaries all over Europe, thousands of tiny transparent 'glass eels' head up river from the sea. Once they get into fresh water, they develop into elvers and start feeding. They spend between five and twenty years in the rivers, developing to yellow eels and then to silver eels. They then head back out to sea to breed. They swim over 6,000 kilometres to the Sargasso Sea off the west coast of America to lay their eggs in the water, and these hatch into tiny larvae, which swim all the way back again – a journey that can take another three years! They change into glass eels and the whole cycle starts again.

Doting dads

Seahorses don't look like fish, but they are and they have a very unusual way of reproducing. It all starts when the male and female spend hours dancing together as part of their courtship. When they're convinced they've found the perfect partner, the female lays her eggs into a pouch a bit like a tiny kangaroo's pouch on the male's tummy. The eggs get fertilised here, so it's the male who gets pregnant and he may have 2,000 babies! Once he gives birth though, he's done his bit, and the babies have to fend for themselves.

Pygmy seahorse.

The pygmy seahorses are tiny and well camouflaged. They are difficult to spot amongst soft corals. Can you spot this one?

Class: Amphibians

Amphibians include frogs, toads and newts. They have moist naked skin through which they can absorb oxygen, as well as lungs when they are adults. They spend time on land and in water, where they lay eggs. The young (tadpoles) live in water, breathe through gills and look like fish, but they then undergo a huge change called metamorphosis. This is when they develop their final body shape.

Spectacular superhero skills

Do not underestimate amphibians. They have a range of powers that would make any superhero envious! Read on to discover some spectacular superhero skills that amphibians possess.

Frogs and toads catch insects by flicking their sticky tongues out at high speed to hit them. Their tongues are attached at the front, not at the back like ours, so they can shoot out very fast.

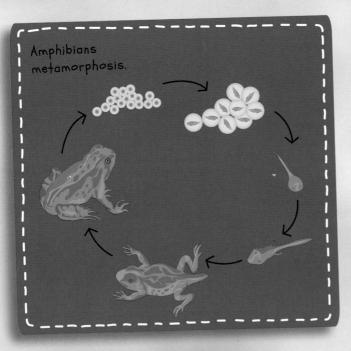

Amphibians metamorphosis.

🐸 Frogs close their eyes when they swallow, not because they're savouring the taste of a delicious fly, but because they use pressure from their eyeballs to help push the food into their throats.

Wood frog in snow.

🐸 Iberian ribbed newts push their own ribs through their skin to make temporary spines if they are attacked. Since they also have toxic skin this discourages a lot of predators from eating them.

🐸 The North American wood frogs can freeze solid in very cold winter weather. Their hearts stop and they can be encased in ice – in other words, they're dead. They can stay like this for weeks, but when they thaw out, they come back to life! They use this incredible ability to survive temperatures as low as -18 degrees Celsius.

🐸 A five centimetre long golden poison dart frog has enough poison on its skin to kill 10-20 people. It may be the most poisonous animal on earth.

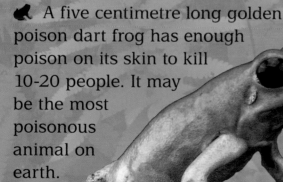

Golden poison dart frog.

Class: Reptiles

Reptiles have dry skin which is covered in scales. They lay leathery-shelled eggs on land. Some live on land and others in water. They include lizards, snakes, turtles, tortoises and crocodiles.

Tortoises and turtles

Tortoises and turtles can live for a very long time. The oldest recorded tortoise was Tu'i Malila, who was reputedly given to the King of Tonga by Captain Cook in 1777. The tortoise was 189 when it died in 1965. In most animals, the gender of a baby depends on what sex chromosomes it has, but in many reptiles, it depends on the temperature at which the eggs develop. Turtle eggs develop into males in cool conditions, and females in warm conditions.

Komodo dragon.

Lizards

The biggest and most fearsome lizard in the world is the Komodo dragon. It can grow to be three metres long and weigh up to 75 kilograms. They are fast and ferocious predators and can attack humans as well as other large animals (including other Komodo dragons), although they will scavenge dead animals too.

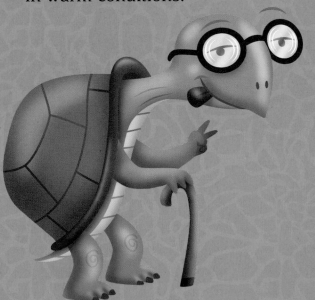

Many chameleons can change their skin colour to blend into the background. They have eyes that can move independently, so they can look in two directions at once, and a long tongue that can shoot out at high speed. These adaptations make them very good hunters.

Snakes

Snakes have two main methods of hunting. Constrictors crush their prey by wrapping themselves around them and squeezing. Some constrictors are huge – anacondas can be over seven metres long, and can go for a year without eating (they would need to eat something pretty big first: the snake equivalent of Christmas lunch).

Boa constrictor.

Venomous snakes kill with a bite. The most venomous one of all is the inland taipan. Some snakes have special areas on their face that allow them to detect infrared radiation from other living things. This means that they can catch and kill prey in total darkness.

Crocodiles and alligators

What's the difference? Alligators are only found in the USA and China. They have wider jaws and darker skin than crocodiles, and are generally only found in fresh water, whereas some crocodiles live in salt water. Saltwater crocodiles are the biggest crocodiles. The largest one on record was 6.1 metres long.

Like turtles, the gender of crocodiles depends on the temperature at which the eggs develop. They will all be female at low or high temperatures, and male at intermediate temperatures.

Class: Birds

Black and white swiftlet.

Cardinal.

Birds have bodies covered in feathers. Their front legs have turned into wings and they have beaks instead of teeth. They can also keep their body temperature stable, independent of the temperature of their surroundings. They breathe using lungs and lay hard-shelled eggs to reproduce.

Fabulous bird facts

Birds range in size from the bee hummingbird with a mass of less than two grams, to the ostrich, which weighs in at over 100 kilograms. The ostrich can't fly, and has very small wings for its size. The biggest wingspan belongs to the wandering albatross, at 3.5 metres. The cassowary is nearly as big as an ostrich, and is probably the most dangerous bird in the world – one kick of its mighty legs can seriously injure someone.

Cassowary.

Speedy!

Birds can move very fast! A peregrine falcon can reach nearly 400 kilometres per hour in a hunting dive and an ostrich can peak at 90 kilometres per hour when it's running. The fastest swimmers are gentoo penguins, which can whizz along underwater at 40 kilometres per hour.

Grey owl.

Cave swiftlets use saliva to glue their nests to the rocks inside caves!

Serious senses

Birds have amazing senses. Some species of owl have feathers on their faces that act a bit like a satellite dish receiver and focus sound. The great grey owl has such good hearing that it can hunt mice hiding under snowdrifts.

Cave swiftlets and oilbirds can avoid obstacles in total darkness by using echolocation (this is a way of detecting objects by bouncing sound waves off them).

Many birds, for instance pigeons, can detect the Earth's magnetic field and use it to navigate. This is how homing pigeons are able to find their way back home.

Class: Mammals

This is the group to which humans belong. Mammals have hairy or furry skin, breathe using lungs and can control their body temperature like birds. The young of most mammals develop inside the uterus of the mother's body and are fed on her milk once they are born. These are called placental mammals.

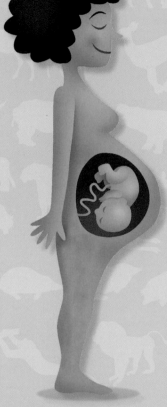

Monotremes

These are mammals which lay eggs instead of giving birth to live young. There are five species – four types of echidna (or Spiny Anteater), and the duck-billed platypus. When scientists first saw a platypus, they thought it must be a hoax! Who would have believed there was an egg laying mammal with a duck's bill, a tail like a beaver, and venomous spurs on its legs?

Marsupials

Marsupials – kangaroos and wombats for example – don't lay eggs, but their young don't develop for very long inside the mother's body. Instead they are born very poorly developed and absolutely tiny (a new born kangaroo only weighs about two grams – about the same as a jelly bean). They have to crawl over the mother's fur all the way to a special pouch where they will stay and grow for several months. All the mammals that are native to Australia are either egg-layers or marsupials, but placental mammals were introduced by ship when humans arrived. These were usually more successful at reproducing, causing the native marsupial species to die out.

Most mammals have four legs which they use to walk or run, and live on land, but of course, there are some exceptions.

Bats

Bats have a web of skin between their front and hind legs that they use as wings. They are brilliant flyers, but useless at getting about on the ground. They fly at night, and rely on their amazing hearing to steer and hunt.

Whales, porpoises and dolphins, oh my!

Whales, porpoises and dolphins are mammals, not fish! Their limbs have turned into flippers and a tail and their bodies have become very streamlined so they can move swiftly through water. The blue whale is the largest animal ever to have lived – it can grow to be 30 metres long and weigh 200 tons. Their tongues weigh as much as a fully grown elephant!

They get to this size on a diet mostly made up of tiny shrimp-like animals called krill, but they do eat up to four tons of them a day. They don't crunch them up with teeth, because they don't have any. Instead they basically have a huge sieve in their mouths, made of a material called baleen.

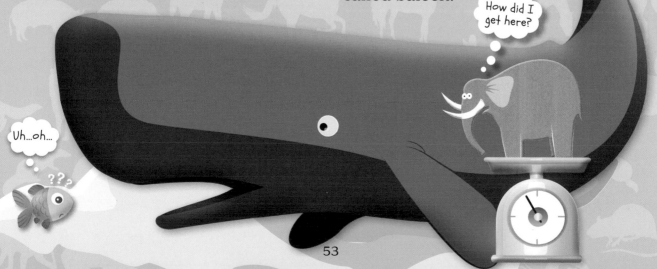

How did I get here?

Uh...oh...

???

Great Apes

Mammals include humans, and our closest relatives among them are the Great Apes: orangutans, gorillas, chimpanzees and bonobos. None of them have tails, even though that is a defining characteristic of a mammal. They do have them as embryos though, when they are developing into babies in their mother's bodies, but they reabsorb them long before they are born, just like a tadpole does when it turns into a frog.

Location of the Great Apes throughout the world.

All Great Apes live in Africa, except the orangutan, which lives in Sumatra and Borneo. They are all endangered species, due to habitat loss, hunting and the effects of civil war. They can all use tools, but chimpanzees and bonobos are best at this. Some apes have been taught to communicate in sign language with people.

The Chimpanzee was the first non-human animal that was recorded using tools.

54

Bonobos

Our closest relatives of all are the bonobos (which used to be called pygmy chimpanzees). We share about 98% of our genetic makeup with them (tigers and domestic cats only share 96% of their genes with each other).

Kanzi, a 26-year-old Bonobo, can use 348 different signs and understands many spoken words. He lives with members of his family in an ape sanctuary with lots of outdoor space, a house that includes a kitchen with a microwave and vending machine which they can operate, and a computer on which they watch DVDs of their choice. If he is given marshmallows and matches, he can build a fire and toast marshmallows on a twig.

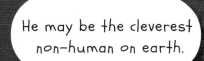

He may be the cleverest non-human on earth.

Bonobos are our distant cousins – and they are very clever.

Humans

We'll end our tour of life on Earth by looking at our own species – *Homo sapiens*. It's easy to think of humans as something special, but are we really any more special than an orchid that pretends to be a wasp, a frog that can survive freezing temperatures, or a bonobo that can toast marshmallows on a fire he's built by himself? And if we are different, what makes us different?

Appearance

Well, we certainly look a bit different from the Great Apes. We are much less hairy, so we wear clothes to stay warm, and we are far more upright when we stand and walk. We aren't as strong as chimpanzees, but our control over our muscles is much more exact, so our movements can be more precise. Our jaws, lips, tongues and the vocal cords in our throats are different to those of the apes as well, and the differences mean we can make a far larger range of sounds. This means humans can communicate very complicated ideas in a spoken language.

Brilliant brains

But it's our brains that really set us apart from our nearest relatives. They are much larger in comparison to our body size than ape brains, and they have many more connections between the various parts. We can think in ways that simply aren't possible for any other species. This allows us to use symbols to communicate – that's what's happening now, as you read the patterns of ink on paper that form this book. It also lets us come up with new ideas, from something as simple as the design of a paperclip, to theories about how life on Earth began...

Wonderful life

Life on Earth is a huge subject to tackle in a book like this. For every organism included here, there are tens of thousands that couldn't be fitted in. The most amazing thing is that every one of them is unique, and wonderful in its own way. Every bacterium, fungus, cactus, wasp and shark – and every other living thing – is fantastically well suited to its own particular way of life. A snail is just as fascinating and beautiful as a tiger, if you look at it properly.

Looking after life

We are the only species that can study other organisms. We are the only species that can try to understand how all the other organisms work and what they need to survive. And we are certainly the only species capable of appreciating how precious all the other ones are.

It's our responsibility to try to look after life on Earth. Not just the cute and cuddly bits, but life in all its scaly, slimy, prickly, squishy glory!

BIOLOGY PLANTS ANIMALS ASTRONOMY

Try It Yourself

Which way is up?

Gardening would take much longer if you had to plant every seed the right way up. We don't usually see what happens to upside-down seeds, because they are underground, but you can find out by doing a simple experiment.

You will need:

• Broad bean seeds
• Sewing pins
• A piece of Oasis block (you can buy this in a florist's or garden centre)
• An empty plastic tub, big enough to hold the Oasis block and leave a bit of space around the sides

What to do:

1. Soak a few beans in water overnight. Soak the Oasis at the same time.
2. The next day, use the sewing pins to fix the beans to the sides of the Oasis block, so that some are the right way up, some are sideways and some are upside down.
3. Put the Oasis block in the tub and add water so it is standing in a shallow pool of water, but the water doesn't reach the beans (or they will rot).
4. Look at the beans every day and watch the roots and shoots change the direction they grow until the roots head down and the shoots head up. Remember to keep the Oasis wet!
5. When you finish the experiment you can plant the beans in a pot of soil or in the garden.

What do woodlice want?

If you look under pots or logs in your garden or school grounds, you might find some woodlice. If you collect some, you can carry out an investigation into what conditions they prefer. Don't worry about picking them up: they won't bite or sting you – they are lovely, and completely harmless.

What you need:

- 10–20 woodlice
- An empty shoebox or big plastic tub
- Some black paper or fabric
- Gravel, dead leaves, sand, soil, small stones — you may be able to think of other things as well.

What to do:

First you can investigate whether your woodlice prefer light or dark. Put them in the shoebox, but don't put the lid on, and let them get used to it for 5-10 minutes. Now cover half the box with the black paper or cloth. Leave the experiment for 20 minutes, then see where the woodlice are. Most of them will probably prefer darkness. Make different areas in your shoebox using the gravel and other substances you have collected. Try to make some damp areas and some dry areas. Release your woodlouse into their hotel and put the lid on the box. Leave them overnight then count how many have chosen each area. Woodlice usually prefer dark and damp conditions, and like to be under cover. This makes sense as it keeps them hidden from animals that would like to eat them, and prevents them from drying out.

Wildlife Expert

You can become a wildlife expert without having to go somewhere exotic!
- If you have a garden, spend some time really getting to know the wildlife there. If not, you could try a nearby field, park or your school grounds.
- Put out bird food and learn to identify the birds that visit your garden. This site will help you work out what bird you're watching: http://www.rspb.org.uk/wildlife/birdidentifier/
- Watch for butterflies and get involved in the next Big Butterfly Count: http://www.bigbutterflycount.org/
- If you see Bumble Bees, there's a great identification guide at: http://www.nhm.ac.uk/nature-online/life/insects-spiders/identification-guides-and-keys/bumblebees/

Find Out More

This book only has space for a very brief introduction to this enormous and wonderful subject. If it has sparked your interest in any sort of living thing, you can easily find out lots more about it.

Visit

Take a trip to a zoo or wildlife park, a butterfly farm or bird of prey centre, an urban farm or botanic garden or nature reserve. If you can't get to any of these, have a look at webcam feeds from zoos all over the world at http://www.thezooonline.com/

Read

My Family and Other Animals by Gerald Durrell. The wonderful true story of animal mad 10-year-old Gerry, who lived on the Greek island of Corfu with his eccentric family for several years. He went on to have his own zoo when he grew up and wrote several more terrific books.

Watch

Anything narrated or presented by David Attenborough. He can enthuse about anything from a blue whale to a head louse, and make you understand how wonderful each of them is!

You can see Kanzi the Bonobo building a fire and toasting marshmallows at www.youtube.com/watch?v=GQcN7lHSD5Y

Log on to

There's lots of good information about pond dipping here http://www.wildlife-man.co.uk/resources.html

There are excellent downloadable identification charts for all sorts of wildlife at http://www.wildlifewatch.org.uk/spotting-sheets

Glossary

AIDS A disease of the immune system that makes it difficult for the body to fight off infections

Amino acids 'Building blocks' used in every cell of the body to build proteins

Anticoagulant Substance that stops blood clotting

Asexual reproduction Organisms producing offspring (new organisms) on their own without the need for both male and female cells

Asteroids Small rocky objects in space that orbit the Sun

Bacteria Simple single-celled organisms that are found all over the world, including in the human body

Bacteriophage Virus that infects and reproduces inside bacteria

Baleen Strong material made out of keratin (the protein that our hair and fingernails are made from)

Cartilage Slippery material that covers the ends of bones and joints

Chlorophyll Green pigment found in plants

Civil war War between groups of people from the same country or state

Classification Putting things into classes or categories

Decomposed Broken down into simple substances

DNA Material in an organism that carries all the information about how it will look and work

Echolocation Making sounds and using the echoes from the sounds to work out where objects are

Eukaryotic cells Cells that contain a nucleus and other parts

Excretion Getting rid of waste products that have been made by an organism

Gamete Cell that fuses with another cell during fertilisation to form a new organism

Genetically modified When organisms have had their DNA changed in a non-natural way

Hermaphrodite Organism with both male and female reproductive organs

Homo sapiens Scientific name for the human species

Infrared Invisible electromagnetic radiation with a wavelength longer than visible light

Irreversible Not possible to change back

Latin An ancient language originally spoken in ancient Rome, but now used for scientific names of organisms

61

Locomotion Movement from place to place

Malaria Often fatal disease carried by mosquitoes, causing a high fever and chills

Metamorphosis Complete change in body form (from young to adult)

Meteorite Rock that falls to Earth from space

Migration Movement of animals from one region to another

Mildew Thin fungus growth

Molecules Groups of atoms (body 'building blocks') bonded together

Multicellular Made up of many different cells

Navigate Find your way around

Nucleus Part of a cell that controls what happens in the cell

Nutrition Getting the food needed for growth and health

Offspring New organisms

Ovule The female reproductive cells of plants

Parasite Organism living in or on another organism, often causing harm to the other organism

Photosynthesis Process used by plants to convert carbon dioxide and water into food, using energy from sunlight

Primordial Very first, earliest

Prokaryotic cells Simple cells that do not contain a nucleus and are only found in bacteria

Proteins Essential part of all living organisms (part of the muscle, skin and bones in humans)

Radiation Energy in the form of electromagnetic waves

Respiration Breaking down food in cells to release energy

Sexual reproduction Organisms producing offspring (new organisms) using both male and female cells that join together

Smallpox Often fatal disease. Those infected have a fever and blisters all over the skin

Spectrum Band or scale

Spore Small, single-celled body that can grow into a new organism

Toxic Poisonous

Venomous Poisonous

Virus Organism that infects cells and reproduces inside them

UV Ultraviolet radiation. Invisible electromagnetic radiation from the Sun with a wavelength shorter than visible light

Introduction

If you're reading this book, then you're a living organism, and assuming you're on Planet Earth, then you're a human. You are also surrounded by countless other types of living things. About 1.4 million species have been named so far, but there may be tens of millions more.

But what exactly *is* life? What is a living thing? What makes a real flower different from an artificial one? If trees and tables are both made of wood, does that mean they're both alive? And what about a woolly jumper? It used to be part of a sheep…

Confused? Don't worry *A Beginner's Guide* will help you understand what life is and take you on a tour of some of the most extraordinary examples of life on Earth.

So, how did life begin?

Turn the page to discover some possible answers…

How Life Began

Planet Earth is around 4,500 million years old. As far as we know, *life* on Earth began about 3,500 million years ago. This is just an estimate, because there was no one around to see it, but scientists have worked out a number of possible ways it could have happened. The theory below is one of the best known.

Primordial soup

Millions of years ago, Earth was very different from the planet we live on now. It's believed that the atmosphere (all of the gases surrounding Earth) was composed of the gases methane, ammonia, hydrogen and water vapour, instead of the mixture of oxygen, nitrogen and carbon dioxide we breathe today. There were no animals or plants, no bacteria, no cells, no forms of life at all. There was just a 'soup' of simple chemicals in the oceans. This is sometimes called 'primordial soup'. (Primordial means the very first, or earliest.)

Life from lightning?

Earth was a very violent planet back then, with volcanic eruptions and huge electrical storms. Bolts of lightning frequently struck the ocean, and high levels of UV light from the sun bombarded it with radiation. This provided energy which allowed the simple chemicals to join together to make more complicated ones. Scientists have carried out experiments that attempt to recreate this, and have found that amino acids – the building blocks from which proteins are made – will form under these conditions.

Eventually, molecules were formed that had the ability to copy themselves. These were related to the DNA found in the cells of all living things today. And so life began.